The Bunker Theatre present

ABIGAIL

by Fiona Doyle

Abigail was first performed at The Bunker, London,
on 10 January 2017

ABIGAIL

by Fiona Doyle

CAST

WOMAN	Tia Bannon
MAN	Mark Rose

CREATIVE TEAM

Director	Joshua McTaggart
Designer	Max Dorey
Lighting Designer	Christopher Nairne
Sound Designer	Andy Josephs
Co-Producer	Zoë Robinson
Co-Producer	Joel Fisher
Production Manager	James Anderton
Photography	Jasper Soloff

CAST

TIA BANNON – WOMAN

Theatre includes: *The Winter's Tale, Pericles* (Shakespeare's Globe); *Camelot:The Shining City* (Sheffield Theatres).

TV includes: *Midsomer Murders* (ITV).

Film includes: *Oxygen & Terror* (Royal College of Art).

Tia trained at RADA and graduated in 2015.

MARK ROSE – MAN

Theatre includes: *King Lear* (Old Vic); *The Trial of Jane Fonda, Frozen* (Park Theatre); *Hangmen* (West End); *The Beaux Stratagem, Port, A Taste of Honey* (National Theatre); *Saturday Night and Sunday Morning* (Royal Exchange, Manchester); *Women Laughing* (Old Red Lion; Off West End Award Nomination for Best Actor); *Twelfth Night* (Grosvenor Park Open Air Theatre).

TV includes: *Coronation Street, Emmerdale* (ITV).

Mark is a founder member of The Blueprint Theatre Company.

PRODUCTION TEAM

FIONA DOYLE – WRITER
Fiona completed the John Burgess Playwriting Course in 2012. Plays include: *Coolatully*, which won the 2014 Papatango New Writing Prize and was produced at the Finborough Theatre that same year; *Deluge*, which won the 2014 Eamon Keane Full-length Play Award and was produced at Hampstead Theatre Downstairs in 2015 – both plays are published by Nick Hern Books.

In 2015 Fiona completed a seven-week attachment at the National Theatre Studio and received the Irish Theatre Institute's inaugural 2015/16 Phelim Donlon Playwright's Bursary and Residency Award.

She was one of the writers for '5 Directors, 5 Plays, 5 Days' at the Young Vic in February 2016 and is currently under commission to Hampstead Theatre, ALRA and National Theatre Connections.

In March 2017, *Coolatully* will receive its US premiere in Washington DC.

JOSHUA MCTAGGART – DIRECTOR
Joshua is the co-founder and Artistic Director of The Bunker. *Abigail* is his inaugural production as Artistic Director.

Directing includes: *Marching on Together* (Old Red Lion); *King of the Fuckin' Castle* (VAULT Festival); *Honest Poverty* (Finborough Theatre Vibrant Festival).

Assistant directing includes: *Coolatully, The Floeurs of Edinburgh* (Finborough); *She Kills Monsters* (Boston Centre for the Arts, USA); *The Lily's Revenge* (American Repertory Theatre, USA).

Joshua trained with Diane Paulus and Shira Milikowsky at Harvard University and the American Repertory Theatre.

MAX DOREY – DESIGNER
Max graduated from the Professional Theatre Design MA at Bristol Old Vic Theatre School in 2012. He was a finalist for the Linbury Prize in 2013 and was a trainee/assistant designer at the RSC in 2013/14.

Set and costume design includes: *LUV* (Park); *The Collector* (Vaults – Off West End Award Nomination for Best Set Design); *Cargo* (Arcola); *Last of the Boys* (Southwark Playhouse); *After Independence* (Arcola); P'YONGYANG (Finborough); *No Villain* (Old Red Lion/Trafalgar 2; Off West End Awards nomination for Best Set Design); *And Then Come the Nightjars* (Theatre503; Off West End Awards and UK Theatre Awards Nomination for Best Set Design); *Teddy* (Southwark Playhouse; Off West End Awards Nomination for Best Set Design); *Lardo, Marching on Together* (Old Red Lion); *Coolatully* (Finborough); *Sleight and Hand* (Edinburgh Fringe).

CHRISTOPHER NAIRNE – LIGHTING DESIGNER

Lighting design for theatre includes: *BU21* (Trafalgar Studios); *LUV, The Buskers Opera* (Park); *Beauty and the Beast* (Watford Palace Theatre); *Home Chat, Coolatully* (Finborough); *Cargo, After Independence, Octagon* (Arcola); *Last of the Boys, This Will End Badly, Johnny Got His Gun* (Southwark Playhouse); *Little Light* (Orange Tree); *Lionboy* (Complicite international tour).

Lighting design for opera includes: *A Fairy Queen, Macbeth* (Iford Arts); *Noye's Fludde, The Adventures of Count Ory* (Blackheath Halls Opera); *Albert Herring, La Calisto* (Hampstead Garden Opera); *Belshazzar* (Trinity Laban Conservatoire); *Vivienne* (Linbury Studio, ROH); *La Bohème* (OperaUpClose, 2012 Olivier Award winner).

Christopher was awarded the Off West End Award for Best Lighting Designer 2016 for *Teddy* at Southwark Playhouse. A full list of credits and portfolio are available on his website: www.christophernairne.co.uk

ANDY JOSEPHS – SOUND DESIGNER

Sound design for theatre includes: *All Aboard* (Electric); *A Little Night Music, Kings of Broadway* (Palace); *You Won't Succeed on Broadway…, Putting it Together, Tell Me on a Sunday* (Olivier nomination, Best Revival); *Scenes from a Marriage* (St James); *Little Voice* (Offie nomination for Best Sound Design); *Sunset Boulevard* (Yvonne Arnaud); *My Fair Lady* 60th Anniversary Concert (St Paul's Church).

As production sound: *No Man's Land* (West End/UK tour); *Kite Runner* (West End); *Kiss Me Kate* (Queens); *Encore* (Adelphi); *A View from the Bridge, Scottsboro Boys* (Young Vic).

Andrew currently runs the sound department at the Almeida Theatre.

ZOË ROBINSON – CO-PRODUCER

In 2014, Zoë founded RIVE Productions with Michael Edwards and Oliver Daw. For Rive, Zoë has produced *Skin a Cat*, the inaugural production at The Bunker, *The Dog, the Night, and the Knife* (Arcola); and *Klippies* (Southwark Playhouse).

Producing credits include: *Lean* (Tristan Bates); *Don't Panic! It's Challenge Anneka* (Summerhall, Edinburgh); Berkoff's *The Messiah* (Bootstrap Bunkers, Dalston); *A Midsummer Night's Dream* (Abney Park Cemetery); *Below the Belt* (Pleasance, Edinburgh); *Believers Anonymous* (Rosemary Branch).

Zoë has previously worked at CBBC, as Early Years Associate Producer at the Lyric Hammersmith, Producer at Bill Kenwright Ltd and currently as Producer for the Polka Theatre dedicated to producing and presenting work for young audiences.

A playground for Ambitious Artists to create work for Adventurous Audiences

The Bunker is a new Off-West End theatre in London Bridge housed in a former underground parking garage. The space has been transformed from its original abandoned state into a unique 110-seater deep beneath the pavements of Southwark Street.

With four concrete pillars marking out the thrust performance space, an eclectic mix of audience seating on three sides of the stage, and a snug bar tucked into the corner of the venue, The Bunker has a unique character that feels both classical and contemporary.

Founded by Artistic Director Joshua McTaggart and Executive Producer Joel Fisher, The Bunker's first season of work opened in October 2016 with *Skin a Cat* by Isley Lynn, an award-winning transfer from VAULT Festival. The Bunker puts artists at the centre of its programming, and the space functions as a gallery as well as a performance space.

Driven by a desire to create theatre that is an event for its audience, The Bunker is attempting to redefine what an evening at the theatre is like. From post-show poetry to pop-up dance performances, from scratch nights to movie nights, there is always something different on offer at The Bunker, but the focus is always the same: an unforgettable evening of entertainment, discovery, and adventure.

Find Out More
You can find out more about The Bunker, our first season, and our other work by visiting our website, calling the box office, or dropping us an email.

Website: www.bunkertheatre.com
Box Office: 0207 234 0486
Email: info@bunkertheatre.com
Address: 53a Southwark Street, London, SE1 1RU

THE BUNKER TEAM

Artistic Director	Joshua McTaggart
Executive Producer	Joel Fisher
Associate Director	Sara Joyce
Technical Manager	Hannah Fisher
Bar Manager	Lee Whitelock

The Bunker could not run smoothly without the incredible work of our volunteer ushers. If you would like to join The Bunker team, then email us on **info@bunkertheatre.com**

OUR SUPPORTERS

The Bunker would like to thank the following individuals for their support in getting The Bunker off the ground and helping us to launch our first season of work:

Philip and Chris Carne, Laurence Isaacson, The Edwin Fox Foundation, Mark Schnebli, Monty Fisher, Charlotte Houghteling, Joscelyn Fox and Lt Cdr Paul Fletcher, Roger Horrell, Melvyn Dubbell, Quay Chu, Paul Slawson-Price, George Arthur, Roger Horrell, Sara Naudi, Felicity Trew, Edward Glover, Matthew Payne, Alex Leung, Barbara Cantelo. The Stephen Sondheim Society, Matt Brinkler, Max Stafford-Clark

As a registered Community Interest Company (Company Number 10330447) that does not receive subsidy, The Bunker relies on generous support from individuals, foundations, and companies to help us make relevant and ambitious theatre. If you would like to support the work that The Bunker creates, you can find out how at **www.bunkertheatre.com/support-us**

ABIGAIL

Fiona Doyle

Acknowledgements

Abigail was one of the first plays I wrote so the response it drew at the time was very encouraging from an emerging-writer point of view. With that in mind, thank you to the Bruntwood Prize for Playwriting, the Eamon Keane Full-length Play Award, Theatre503, Diyan Zora, Thomas Conway, and Will Mortimer. Thank you also to the actors Charlie De Bromhead and Kathryn O'Reilly for taking part in a read-through of an earlier draft. And thanks in particular to Joshua McTaggart, Sarah Joyce and all at The Bunker who took the 'nearly there' play and made it happen.

F.D.

'Time present and time past
Are both perhaps present in time future,
And time future contained in time past.'

'Burnt Norton', Four Quartets,
T.S. Eliot

4

Characters

MAN, *mid-forties*
WOMAN, *mid-twenties*

Note on Text

A forward slash (/) indicates the point where the immediately following dialogue, or action, interrupts.

A dash (–) indicates the point where a line of dialogue is abruptly cut off by the speaker themselves or by something/ someone else.

An ellipsis (…) indicates a hesitation, a thought changing track, being lost for words.

The absence of a punctuation mark at the end of a line interrupted by a forward slash (/) indicates that the line of dialogue would have continued if there had been no interruption.

This text went to press before the end of rehearsals and so may differ slightly from the play as performed.

Darkness.

A piercing sound.

It increases in volume, getting louder and louder until…

1. Kitchen

MAN *is sitting at table. He is unshaven, barefoot and dressed casually. There's a half-empty beer bottle in front of him.* WOMAN *is wearing a smart black dress and she is looking at him.*

Silence.

WOMAN. Why aren't you dressed?

MAN. There was snow when we landed.

   Beat.

   You had snow in your hair. Walking to the terminal. / There was snow.

WOMAN. Put some socks on.

MAN. Unseasonal weather patterns. (*Smiles.*) D'you remember? There was something strange going on alright.

   Beat.

   You let that taxi go and I knew then. When you let / that taxi go.

WOMAN. They won't hold the table.

MAN. Berlin still reminds me of you. With snow in your hair.

   Beat.

So we got the next one together. You were looking out the window at the snow. And you joked about the plane coming down. Remember? You joked about it. Weren't we lucky the plane hadn't crashed. Weren't we lucky we hadn't crashed in a snowstorm. And you looked at me and smiled. You'd a beautiful smile. I knew I'd spend a long time with you then. I knew we'd go past that. Through it. Out the other side into a life together, y'know?

Pause.

WOMAN. Don't.

MAN. You've a beautiful smile.

WOMAN. You can't.

MAN. I'm sorry I couldn't make you smile more.

WOMAN....

MAN. Things start. Then they end –

WOMAN. Try again –

MAN. I tried. I did.

WOMAN. / Try again.

MAN. But I can't undo it. I can't undo what we've done, what we've –

WOMAN. We?

Silence.

MAN. It all passes. This has passed.

They look at each other. WOMAN *suddenly breaks a plate. He stares at the pieces for a moment, then exits. She stands there frozen to the spot.*

2. Airport, Berlin

WOMAN *is standing in the snow waiting for a taxi.* MAN *enters and stands beside her.*

MAN. Might be a while. Before another one comes.

WOMAN. What? I…

Pause.

MAN. What's your name again?

WOMAN. I remember yours.

Beat.

MAN. You look like a Kate. You a Kate?

WOMAN *shakes her head.*

Not a Kate. Alice? Not Kate, not Alice. Grace?

She shakes her head.

Helen?

Same.

Joanna? Martina? Tracey?

WOMAN. Tracey?

Beat.

No.

MAN. Tell me.

WOMAN. Again.

MAN. Tell me again.

WOMAN. I'll think about it.

They wait.

MAN. I'm just here for work. Not on my list of places to see before I die, y'know?

WOMAN. You have a list?

MAN. I have a list. It's a long list. Great Wall of China for starters. Then Chichén Itzá, / then

WOMAN. Where?

MAN. Ancient Mayan city. Mexico. There's this temple right, and if you get there at the right time of year, when the sun and the earth are –

WOMAN. Equinox?

MAN. That's the one. So if you're there for an equinox this shadow appears. This long dark shadow and it attaches itself to a serpent's head sitting at the base of the pyramid. This... serpent's head made of stone. Perfectly aligned. Same time every year for thousands of years. Incredible. So that's definitely on the list. Great Wall of China, Chichén Itzá, Petra, Ayers Rock –

WOMAN. Where's Petra?

MAN. Jordan. Huge palaces carved into the mountainside. It's a long list.

They wait.

Hands not cold?

WOMAN. A bit.

MAN (*removing his gloves and offering them to her*). Here.

WOMAN. Won't yours be now?

MAN. I'll live.

She puts them on.

Too early for snow. Unseasonal weather patterns is what they're saying. Very strange. (*Starts humming quietly.*) Been stuck in my head all day long.

They look at each other. He leans in. She laughs.

…

WOMAN. Sorry. You just… sort've reminded me of someone. Just for a moment.

MAN. Can I kiss you?

WOMAN. You can't even remember my name.

Pause. He leans in. She starts laughing again.

MAN. Oh c'mon now!

WOMAN. Sorry, sorry. K. Right.

Beat.

I'm ready.

3. Bedroom (Part 1)

MAN *stands looking out of window, back to audience.*
WOMAN *stands behind him with a beer bottle.*

MAN (*without turning*). I have a pain in my head.

WOMAN. Forgot your beer. Don't you want it? We're meant to be celebrating.

She holds it out. He doesn't turn around.

You used tell me I was beautiful.

Beat.

Like marble you said.

Beat.

You said / that.

MAN. Yes, I said that, I said that. A long time ago.

Pause.

WOMAN. Where will you go? Home? Up north? Fucking… Chitzy whereverthefuck.

MAN. Chichén Itzá? (*Laughs a little.*) Forgot about that.

WOMAN. Well go on then. What you waiting for.

MAN. An equinox.

WOMAN. Right.

MAN (*to himself*). Need an equinox.

WOMAN. Hope it rains. I do, I hope it rains on you. Shadow won't be there if it rains.

MAN. Shadow won't be there 'cause it's the wrong time of year –

WOMAN *screams*.

Silence.

He turns and looks at her like she's a stranger.

In the Louvre, there's a statue of Aphrodite. Goddess of love and beauty. 100 BC. Six foot high. Beautiful. But her arms are missing. She has no arms. Part of her is gone. Still beautiful. But there's a bit of her missing that she can't ever get back. Not her fault. Not her fault she was buried and forgotten about. In a field. For centuries. They found her in a field. Some farmer. Digging. Found her in the mud so he dug her up. Without her arms. Covered in muck and grime. I wonder… I wonder if he thought she was beautiful then. Probably not. Probably not 'til he washed the mud off her. Probably didn't know she was beautiful 'til the dirt was gone. He could never be entirely sure until the dirt was gone.

Pause.

I feel a bit weak.

Darkness.

Piercing sound again.

Then a heart beating a little too fast.

The sounds mix together, the heartbeat increasing in pace, until…

4. Pre-Christmas

MAN *and* WOMAN *are both sat in front of a laptop.* MAN *is scrolling down.*

MAN. Thailand? Good value, cheap flights, great weather –

WOMAN. Too long.

MAN. What?

WOMAN. Too long a flight for just a week.

MAN. Oh. K.

She starts to type.

Egypt? Pyramids, Valley of the Kings? Although. Friend've mine said the Pyramids were a big let-down. Full of crap. Other people's crap. Coke cans, sweet wrappings, camel shit everywhere. They just wander round pissing and shitting everywhere.

WOMAN. How 'bout... here?

They look at the screen.

MAN. That's on my list.

WOMAN (*scrolling*). I know.

MAN. You a hiker then?

WOMAN. I like to walk.

MAN. A Christmas hike.

WOMAN. Something different.

Beat.

MAN. Why you so weird about me meeting them?

WOMAN. I'm not.

MAN. You are.

WOMAN. I think we should book this.

Beat.

MAN. Seriously, will I ever –

WOMAN. You're pushing at me, don't… push at me.

He looks at her for a moment. She's still focused on the screen.

MAN. I'm not –

WOMAN (*turning to face him*). When you push at me like that it makes my stomach twist, I go all hot, I can't think straight –

MAN. Alright, alright. Jesus.

Pause.

WOMAN. I… I'm just tired. And my back is sore.

They return focus to the screen. He rubs her back.

MAN. Can I ask you one thing. Just one right? Is it the age difference?

She rolls her eyes.

You worried what they'll think –

WOMAN. No! I don't care what they think, can think what they like, I just… I hate this time of year. I actually really fucking hate it so I want to go away. With you. Have a nice time.

MAN. K.

WOMAN. Okay?

MAN. Fine.

Pause.

WOMAN. It's not good for me to be too close to them, some people… that's just the way it is.

He nods.

She starts typing something in.

MAN. Thing is though, they're part of you. And I want to know all the parts of you.

WOMAN (*turns and looks at him*). You don't.

MAN. …

WOMAN. You don't.

She turns back to the screen and continues typing. He tucks a stray piece of hair behind her ear.

5. Bedroom (Part 2)

MAN *and* WOMAN *stand facing each other.*

WOMAN. Do you like my dress? It's new. It's a new dress. Feels nice against my skin. Expensive.

Beat.

If I'd known you were going to let me down like this... would've gone to yoga but now I'll just be late. I was late last time too and everyone was looking at me and then I couldn't find a space for my mat and... look, would you... would you like me to make some dinner here instead? We can celebrate here if you... you'll have to do the washing up though. 'Cause it's your turn. And make sure you rinse. Suds should be rinsed away. It's not clean otherwise. Sometimes you don't even scrub off the food crust. On the inside of the saucepan? You just... scrub round the outside and along the rim but you forget to scrub the inside. Were you never shown? How to scrub the inside?

MAN. I'm leaving you.

Beat.

D'you hear me?

Beat.

I'm leaving / you.

WOMAN. You're too old to leave.

MAN. I'm leaving –

WOMAN. You've not been taking care of yourself have you. That's why you look / so pale

MAN. I'm done / with all this.

WOMAN. You've not been eating properly. You've not been taking care of me and you've not / been taking care of yourself.

MAN. I can't fix this. It's gone too far. I can't fix this and I can't fix you –

WOMAN. I don't need fixing, I need you to do the / washing up!

MAN. You drive me crazy, I drive you crazy, we're stained now, we're… we're dirty. And I need it to be clean. But it can't be and it won't ever be again!

Beat.

WOMAN. My hands are dry. I should moisturise more –

MAN. Christ's sake.

He makes a move to go. She raises the beer bottle in her hand. He stops.

Seriously?

She keeps it held high.

Silence.

WOMAN. How about a stir-fry. Quick. Easy. That okay for you?

Beat.

You really do look ill.

He just stares at her. Her arm is still raised, bottle gripped tightly.

6. Christmas

MAN *and* WOMAN *are hiking up a steep hill. A thick fog has rolled in.* MAN *is out of breath.*

WOMAN. You sure you don't –

MAN. I said I'm fine.

WOMAN. But maybe you / need to

MAN. Would you please just... okay? I'm –

WOMAN. Alright. Okay. We're here now anyway. This is it, this is – damn.

They both look around for a few moments.

I can feel it. I can feel how beautiful it is but I – I can't see anything.

MAN. Sounds like a long way down.

WOMAN. I can't see anything.

Pause.

MAN. Look, can we talk about –

WOMAN. S'like being in a dream.

MAN. I think / we need to

WOMAN. Like being awake inside a dream –

MAN. That wasn't... it wasn't me. What happened. Last night, I –

WOMAN. I know, it was my fault –

MAN. No, there were two of us, but –

WOMAN. This was all a huge waste of time wasn't it.

MAN. What?

WOMAN. This holiday. This hike. Hiking all the way up here to... and now we're here, we've made it, but there's just fog. There's just this goddamn fog everywhere making me dizzy, making us...

Beat.

MAN. Said you can feel it though. You can feel it, so…

They look at each other.

We'll get over it right? Last night? Bit heated but…

WOMAN. If we stop looking back. Can we stop looking back?

Pause.

MAN (*pointing down*). Clearing there, see?

WOMAN. Where?

MAN. There, just caught a glimpse of… oh. S'gone again.

WOMAN. Changes so quickly –

MAN. I saw the shape of something. And the sea. The waves. Proper long way down. (*Bending down.*) Hey, look at this. Didn't think these grew here. (*Picks one and gives it to her.*) Poisonous y'know.

WOMAN. They're not.

MAN. Blister your skin if you hold them too long. Nasty taste mind so only a fool would eat them but then the world's full of fools. D'you know what happens if you swallow one?

She shakes her head.

First your mouth starts to burn. Then the inside of your throat as it makes its way down your digestive tract. Start to feel a bit nauseous. Bit confused. Dizzy maybe. Might throw up if you've eaten a good few. If you're a real fool and you've swallowed a load, you won't be able to breathe. (*Playing up the dramatics.*) You'll start shaking. Convulsing like a lunatic in the madhouse, like someone's put their hand around your throat, squeezing the life out of you, like you're being strangled from the inside.

Beat.

And then you die.

WOMAN (*looking at it*). Thought all they did was tell you who likes butter.

MAN. Surrounded by danger. Foxgloves over there? Poisonous.
Passed some water hemlock earlier? Poisonous. Ferns?
Poisonous. Ragworth? Poisonous. Oak trees? Poisonous –

WOMAN. Oak trees?

MAN. Well. For horses. Yet to see a human nibbling on one.
But you / never know.

WOMAN. I need to tell you something.

MAN. What?

WOMAN. I… I'm not completely sure yet but…

MAN. …

She looks at him.

Tell me.

Darkness.

Sound of glass shattering into hundreds of tiny pieces.

Blood rushing through vessels.

Then…

7. Bedroom (Part 3)

MAN *is sitting on the floor. His head is bleeding and he's in
shock.* WOMAN *is sweeping up bits of broken bottle.*

WOMAN. Glass everywhere now. Bits've it are… damn it.
Dangerous this. Mind how you go when you get up. I'll try
my best but… bits've it everywhere. (*Tries to pick a splinter
out of the carpet.*) Fuck. (*Looks at her finger, tries to pick it
out.*) Gone deeper now.

Beat.

Take it out. Please. It hurts.

*He looks at her a moment. Then beckons her over. She goes
to him and he removes the splinter for her.*

Thank you. (*Sucks her finger like a child. Then continues clearing the glass.*) When I was small I had a splinter in my toe. Dad tried to get it out with a needle but he couldn't. Poked and prodded around for an age but it wouldn't budge. So next he tried tweezers. Kept digging and digging but… must've been deep. He hadn't realised how deep. So he made me soak my foot in the tub for half an hour. Water was lovely. Nice and warm. Just right. When the time was up, he took me out and sat me on a chair. I could hear a dog barking outside. And then he started sucking. Put his mouth over it and sucked. It tickled. Didn't like it. But he kept on sucking. Closed my eyes and pretended I was at the seaside. Pretended I was paddling in the water and a fish was nibbling at my foot. His hands were big and rough and his mouth felt hot. I didn't like it. I never… then he stopped. Tried the tweezers. It came out. Big long thing. Ugly. Must've been deep. Started gushing blood.

Pause.

MAN. I need to go now.

WOMAN. Is that a gut feeling? Is it? 'Cause your gut feelings are never wrong / are they.

MAN. Fuck you.

Pause.

WOMAN. You can't go if you're hurt. And you're bleeding. That's blood.

Pause.

Forget the stir-fry. I'll make us something good. I'll make us steak and chips. Hand-cut chips the way you like them. A special treat for a special night. It only happens once a night like tonight. Let's start over. Start fresh. That film's on later. The one you like, what's it called? The Western with what's-his-name in it? And that woman. The famous one? All set in one day. You know. The one where the good guy takes on the bad guys all on his own.

Beat.

You can't go. You can't go if you're hurt.

Darkness.

A slowing heartbeat.

Then the sound of a car approaching.

The sweep of headlights reveals the WOMAN *who is blinded by the light. She blocks her eyes.*

The heartbeat and the sound of the car engine get louder and louder until…

8. Hallway

WOMAN *is sitting in a hallway on some stairs. It's very dimly lit. Front door unlocks and* MAN *enters.*

MAN. Why's it so –

WOMAN. Leave it.

MAN. I can't fucking / see anything.

WOMAN. I said leave it.

MAN. Thought you didn't like the dark.

    Beat.

    How long you been sitting there.

WOMAN. You shouldn't drink and drive.

MAN. How long –

WOMAN. Could've killed someone.

    Beat.

    Since you left.

MAN. That was (*Looks at watch.*) four hours ago.

WOMAN. Didn't think you'd come back –

MAN. Well I did.

    Beat.

WOMAN. You lost it.

MAN. 'Cause I'm sick of this. I'm sick of… this isn't me.

WOMAN. / 'Should always listen to your gut.'

MAN. It's all the time now. It's too much, it's too soon –

WOMAN. We both lost it.

Pause.

MAN (*stepping towards her*). Look, I didn't mean –

WOMAN. Don't come near me.

MAN. What?

WOMAN. Don't come any closer.

MAN *notices something.*

MAN. What is that?

WOMAN. Didn't you hear / me?

MAN. What is all that?

WOMAN. I said we lost it. You don't listen do you. You never really… hear me.

MAN. …

WOMAN. It's gone away.

MAN (*stepping closer*). Jesus Ch/rist.

WOMAN. DO NOT TOUCH ME.

Pause.

MAN. You've been sitting in – sitting there like that all this time?

Beat.

Should I call someone? Who should I call? Tell me what to do. I don't know what to do so you'll have to tell me. Did it hurt? Are you / in pain?

WOMAN. I need sleep.

MAN. Okay then. Alright. Let's get you up –

WOMAN. Your brain is more alert when you're asleep. Did you know that? More than when you're awake. So really, we're more awake when we're asleep than when we're awake.

MAN. Can you stand?

WOMAN. Can I stand?

MAN. Yes. Can you stand up?

WOMAN. I...

MAN. Let me help you. Let me do something, I feel so fucking...

She considers him for a moment, then nods. He helps her up slowly.

Tell me what you need.

WOMAN. I need you to take me back.

MAN. Back where?

WOMAN. In time. I need you to take me back in time.

Beat.

MAN. You need sleep. We'll talk after. You need to rest now.

She looks at him and smiles. Then she starts hitting him, beating his chest. He grabs her arms to restrain her and she collapses into him. He holds her until she stops. Silence. She untangles herself and leaves.

Silence.

Christ.

9. Bedroom (Part 4)

MAN *is sitting in same place on floor. Head thrown back against wall looking at the ceiling. The door unlocks from outside and* WOMAN *enters. She sits on the bed.*

WOMAN. Can you stand up?

    Pause.

    Can you?

MAN (*without moving or looking at her*). I hate who I am with you.

WOMAN. That's just you. With or without / me.

MAN. No, it's just – it's just with you. Some of the things we've – some of the things I've done, I've never… we're bad for each other.

    Beat.

    D'you hear me? Are you even…

    Pause.

    What time's it?

WOMAN. Hmm?

MAN. What time is it?

WOMAN. Six fifteen.

MAN. What time's that class?

WOMAN. Seven.

MAN. Then there's still time. You won't be late. I think you should go.

WOMAN. Six fifteen.

MAN. You like that class. Don't you want to go? There's still time.

WOMAN (*slightly trancelike*). They told me I should stay. But there was a machine somewhere. In the hospital, when he was… and I knew he was. I knew. Six fifteen. The time.

When I looked. 'Should've stayed.' That's what they said. They all said I should've… but I… it was a short walk. To the machine. Past all the rooms. All the people. All the same. Sick. Dying. One of them… looked at me. Must've heard my footsteps. He was expecting me. So I stopped and looked back. And he smiled. He smiled at me. Little old man in his bed. Thin. Withering away. Called me 'Mary'. He was so happy to see his Mary. But why had I taken so long?

Beat.

Six thirty-two. 'Shouldn't've gone,' they said. But I wanted a coffee. There was definitely a machine somewhere. Round the corner I saw a boy in a red jumper sat on the floor. All on his own. Playing with a toy car. Blue. Yellow stripes. He looked happy.

Beat.

Seven ten. My foot was asleep and the boy was gone. I'd sat down to watch him and must've… he was going then. 'Stopped breathing at seven twenty,' they said. I think that's when I was getting coffee. Two pound fifty. From a machine! Seven thirty-five. When I got back. Without the coffee. Threw it down a sink on the way there. Didn't taste right. He was still warm. They told me to kiss him goodbye so I did. His skin felt… different. They were all… all tears and collapsed faces. All around him. Like a king. A cold clammy king.

Pause.

Shame. I should never have thrown it away. All it needed was some sugar.

Darkness.

Clocks ticking; a multitude of different ticking sounds.

Heavy, fast breathing.

The sounds mix together and increase in volume.

A sudden gasp for breath, then it all cuts out abruptly.

10. Hotel

MAN *is taking a shower.* WOMAN *is wrapped in a duvet, examining her face in a hand-held mirror.*

WOMAN (*to her reflection*). I think... I think I've changed my mind now.

MAN (*from bathroom*). Sorry?

WOMAN. I... nothing.

MAN. Thought I heard you say something.

WOMAN. No, I was just...

MAN exits from bathroom wrapped in towel.

MAN. First sign of madness that.

He smiles.

She smiles.

He starts pulling on his clothes.

Nice hotel room. Very swish. (*Searches for his top.*) I never do this. Pick up girls like this.

WOMAN. Right.

MAN. I swear. Or at least not lately. There was just... something though, wasn't there?

Beat.

Always listen to your gut, that's what I say –

WOMAN. Listen, I need to... (*Almost a whisper.*) I need to tell you something.

He looks at her.

I didn't think I'd be going back. I didn't think I'd ever leave. I can't afford all this but I thought... it was meant to be permanent. The holiday.

Beat.

D'you understand what I'm –

MAN. Yeah. Yes.

Beat.

A permanent holiday.

She nods.

Pause.

Max out your credit card then?

She nods.

'Cause you didn't think you'd have to pay it back.

She nods.

Beat.

Then they laugh.

Pause.

Why? Why would you…

WOMAN. 'Cause I feel lost. All the time. In this world.

MAN. We all feel lost somet/imes.

WOMAN. Don't do that.

MAN. Do what?

WOMAN. Compare what I feel to what you feel. You can't ever know enough to make that comparison.

Pause.

MAN. I think we're all born with a basic instinct to survive. No matter what. Don't you?

Beat.

You're beautiful.

WOMAN. My teeth are crooked.

MAN. Love the shape of your lips.

WOMAN. My eyes are too big.

MAN (*picks up the mirror and positions it in front of her*). See that? Do ya? D'you see what I see in there?

WOMAN. I don't know.

MAN. Well I think you need to try.

WOMAN. I feel confused now.

MAN. You were laughing a minute ago. Laughing. Think about it.

Pause.

He continues dressing.

WOMAN (*into mirror*). When I was small, I thought dead people lived in them. Thought if you looked hard enough, you could see through to their world. Like a window. (*Looks at him.*) There's a graveyard near here I want to visit. Would you like to come?

11. Bedroom (Part 5)

WOMAN *is looking in a mirror.* MAN *is still sitting on the floor. He is slumped over a little and humming the same song he was humming in Scene 2. Light outside is fading.*

MAN. Same song. Remember? Stuck in my head. Came out of nowhere and now it's stuck. How apt – (*Laughs a little.*) Happy one-year anniversary darling. Happy one or two months of pretty nice stuff followed by ten months of shit. Ten months of utter shit and denial until we arrived (*Gesturing to the room they're in.*) here.

WOMAN (*still looking into mirror*). You're cruel when you want to be.

MAN. Oh I'm cruel. I'm cruel?

WOMAN. I look old. Lines. New ones. Look.

MAN. Can't fucking see you properly can I.

He scratches at his bare foot. She switches on a bedside lamp. It emits a soft glow, not too bright.

WOMAN. Don't like the dark. It's good for hiding in. And why would you need to hide unless something's wrong.

MAN. My mouth feels all dry.

WOMAN. Never liked the dark. Thought things hid in my room. I'd keep my arms under the duvet. Hated going to the toilet. Had to count to three first. Then I'd run. I'd run down the corridor switching all the lights on along the way. Once, I woke to find him sitting on my bed. He whispered that he wanted me to see something. It was Christmas Eve so... so I got up and went with him to the window. I was wearing a nightdress. Pale blue. No underwear. He pushed the curtain back. The moon outside was bright. And then I saw it. For the first time. Snow. Big, white flakes. Falling through the black. Quiet. Soft. He put his arm around me. My shoulders were bare. Could feel his skin. It was so quiet. And dark.

Beat.

Then I felt cold. 'Cause he'd opened it. He'd opened the window and let all the cold in.

Silence.

MAN. When we first met... I should have thought it. I should've just... fucking thought it.

WOMAN. See that lamp? That's like my lamp. Back then. I'd put it on to make the dark go away but I knew that if I turned it off again the dark would still be there. Because when it's dark... it's dark. We can pretend it's not, but... and there's nothing we can do about that.

Beat.

'Cause when it's dark, it's dark.

Darkness.

The sound of a thousand birds fills the auditorium.

The sound builds to a crescendo and then fades until...

12. St Matthäus Kirchhof Cemetery, Berlin

MAN *and* WOMAN *stand before the graves of the Grimm Brothers. A solitary bird sings intermittently throughout the scene.* MAN *is eating a doughnut.*

MAN. You sure? Good doughnut. S'got pretzels in it.

She shakes her head. He gestures to the doughnut.

Berliner. S'what they call 'em. So when Kennedy called himself a Berliner in front of all them people he was really just calling himself a jelly doughnut.

WOMAN. They're not known as Berliners here. They say Pfannkuchen instead so actually, someone from Berlin would have known exactly what he meant.

MAN. You speak German?

WOMAN. Not really, just some words and phrases. Important ones like '*Bitte helfen Sie mir*' 'cause you never know when you might need some help. Burial or cremation?

MAN. Huh?

WOMAN. Which would you want?

MAN. I dunno.

He finishes the doughnut.

WOMAN (*looking at the headstones*). When my father died, my uncles wanted to cremate him but my aunts wanted a grave.

MAN (*looking at her*). I'm sorry.

WOMAN. I didn't care either way. (*Looks at him.*) Why?

MAN. What?

WOMAN. You just said you were sorry. Why?

MAN. For your… for your loss.

WOMAN. Oh.

Beat.

In the end he was cremated.

Pause. Birdsong.

MAN. Have to admit, as far as graveyards go this one's pretty fucking cool.

WOMAN. On my list.

MAN. See? Everyone has one.

WOMAN. I've always liked graveyards. I think they make you feel more alive.

MAN. Basic aren't they? The headstones. For two such famous blokes. D'you've a favourite?

WOMAN. *Hansel and Gretel.*

MAN. That's a scary one I think. For a small kid. Kill the witch in the end don't they?

WOMAN. Shove her in an oven. Burns to death. But I think they should've killed the father too. I mean, he abandoned them didn't he. You don't do that. You don't take your kids into a forest and just leave them there. In the dark. With wild things. That's bad parenting.

MAN. Can't have kids murdering their own parents in a fairytale.

WOMAN. Why not? They kill the witch don't they. The witch might be somebody's mother but just 'cause she is doesn't mean she's not bad. Just 'cause she's somebody's mother.

Beat.

MAN. Well. People are complicated. No one's all good or all bad, we're mostly just a little bit've both.

She looks at him.

WOMAN. You have something here. (*Wipes a crumb away from the corner of his mouth with her fingers.*) So... would you say you're more good than bad then? Or more bad than good?

MAN (*thinks for a moment*). First one I think. Yeah. More good I'd say.

She smiles.

Darkness. Heavy, laboured breathing.

Then...

13. Bedroom (Part 6)

MAN *looks significantly weaker now. His breathing has changed.*

WOMAN. Don't call me that –

MAN. Well where is it then?

WOMAN. You'd miss me. And you need me. You need me to take care of you –

MAN. / Where is it.

WOMAN. I mean, how can you just stop. That must make... I've helped liars before and I shouldn't have.

MAN. My throat feels tight.

WOMAN. Like you've eaten a buttercup? Tight like that? Used think they were beautiful 'til you told me they were poison. Water? I'll go get some but you have to stop all this. D'you think I like it? Hurts me as much as / it hurts you.

MAN. You are. You're mad. You're a mad / little bitch.

WOMAN. I said don't call me that!

Starts raining outside.

Did you know that the Salem witches ate rye grain.

MAN. What the fuck are you on about now.

WOMAN. Rye grain. Know what the cold and the wet does to rye grain? Makes it grow a fungus. Then the fungus produces a hallucinogenic. Like LSD. So they weren't mad. They just had food poisoning. They were being poisoned by something but they killed them anyway.

Beat.

There's poison all round us. I see that now. I'm not mad, I just... see.

Pause.

MAN. Do I remind you of him?

Beat.

Berlin. First kiss in the snow. You laughed 'cause you said I reminded you of... Jesus Christ, do I fucking remind you of him?

Beat. Then he laughs a little.

He did a very good job of you, d'you know that. A very good job.

Silence.

Stop looking at me like that, this is your fault, you've fucking driven / me to it.

WOMAN. How can you say you love someone and then just stop –

MAN. Because things change! They pass! They end! And you need help –

WOMAN. Everyone needs someone to love. Everyone / wants to be loved.

MAN. Everyone wants to be fucking saved! People want saving! You thought I'd save you and I can't. I can't, d'you understand? You're playing games with me now.

WOMAN (*to herself*). 'I love you, I save you.' 'I love you, I save you.' (*Looks at him.*) It is a game isn't it. It's all just one big game. Except this time, I'm winning.

Darkness.

Sound of music playing.

Sound changes and distorts, eventually turning into the sound from a car radio...

14. Taxi

MAN *and* WOMAN *are in the back of a taxi. Radio is on. Street lights flash by as the lights dim outside.*

Long pause.

WOMAN. What d'you think's gonna happen?

MAN. When?

WOMAN. Us. The future.

MAN. Who knows. A surprise.

> *Driver tunes in another station. We hear a new song or perhaps a news bulletin in German.*

WOMAN. If you grew old with me, I'd –

MAN. If I grew old with you?

WOMAN. Yeah.

MAN....

WOMAN. I'd take care of you. When you're old. 'Cause you'll be old before I am.

MAN. Right. Good to know that when I'm pissing in my pants, you'll be there.

WOMAN. I would be.

MAN. Excellent. And apologies in advance for the burden I shall inevitably become. Also, can you please not feed me Complan or Vitalan or any of that shit? In fact, I want that in writing.

WOMAN. K.

MAN. Great.

WOMAN. Vitalan is dog food by the way.

MAN. Look, it's just... not something I think we need to... y'know? Early days.

> *Beat.*

> I'll get this.

> *He rummages for the taxi fare.*

WOMAN. I cared for my father when he got sick. People said I took on too much but... s'what you do when you love someone isn't it. Take care of them.

MAN. I think 'love' is code for 'save'.

WOMAN. What?

MAN. I think, what people mean to say when they say 'I love you' is 'I save you'.

WOMAN. I save you?

MAN. People have a deeply embedded need to be saved from their own lives. S'just nobody wants to admit it.

WOMAN. That's what you think?

MAN (*still rummaging for the right fare*). That's what I think.

WOMAN (*looks at him*). Hey.

MAN. Hmm?

WOMAN. I save you.

He smiles.

MAN. Will you hold my hand on the plane too? Fucking hate flying.

15. Bedroom (Part 7)

Darkness has fallen. MAN *is now lying on the floor motionless.* WOMAN *is looking out of the window.*

WOMAN. I see a man. Out there. Through his window. Through my window. I see him. He can't see me. He doesn't know I'm watching. He's sitting in his armchair and he's looking at something. The light is dim. Can't see what he's looking at. Telly? Person? He's not talking. His lips are still. Maybe he's looking at a picture. A photo of someone. Or something. And it makes him feel good. Or maybe he's just staring. Maybe he's gone into a world inside his brain and his body is just… waiting for him to come back. Don't know. Can't see. I see him but I can't see all of him. And he doesn't see me. (*Looks at* MAN.) You really do look ill. (*Goes and sits on bed. Silence.*) This hurts me. To see you like this. I could've helped but you wouldn't let me. And you wouldn't help yourself. So this is all your fault. But you can't see that can you.

Pause.

I was a little girl. (*Looks at* MAN.) How could you.

Pause.

Missed yoga again. For nothing. They'll think I'm not coming back. Class'll be over now. Exercise is important. I always feel better after.

Pause.

Why? Can you hear me? Are you in there? Can you tell me?

She goes to him. She sits with him for a while. She strokes his face gently. She kisses his forehead.

I'm sorry. (*Stands. Looks out the window before she goes.*)

That man… he's gone now.

Darkness.

A piercing sound.

The sound increases in volume and starts to distort, eventually turning into the sound of a plane's engine coming in for landing…

16. The Beginning

An airport in London. WOMAN *is looking at departure
screens.* MAN *enters. He sits. He takes out a syringe needle
and injects. She watches him. He sees her watching.*

MAN. Diabetes. Type 1. Insulin shots.

She sits.

ANNOUNCER. Attention all passengers travelling on flight
773 to Berlin. There will be a minor departure delay due to
poor weather conditions outside. The ground crew are
currently in the process of de-icing the wings and your flight
should be boarding in approximately thirty minutes from
now. Please listen for further announcements and apologies
for any inconvenience caused.

Pause.

MAN. Strange thing to say.

WOMAN. Sorry?

MAN. Strange thing to say.

WOMAN. ...

MAN. 'Due to poor weather conditions outside.'

Beat.

Hardly due to poor weather conditions inside.

WOMAN. Right.

Silence. He puts the syringe away.

MAN. Ice on the wings. No good that.

WOMAN. What?

MAN. Ice. No good.

WOMAN. Oh. No.

MAN. Not on the wings.

WOMAN. No.

Beat.

Well. They'll remove it won't they. So.

MAN. So you think it'll be fine 'so'?

WOMAN. They won't put a plane full of people in the sky with ice on the wings will they.

MAN. And you trust them? Total strangers? People we can't even see?

WOMAN. No choice.

MAN. Right.

Beat.

Holiday?

WOMAN. Sort of.

MAN. A 'sort of' holiday?

WOMAN. Really none of your business.

Silence.

MAN. I like your lips.

WOMAN. Excuse me?

MAN. Your lips. I like them. The shape of them.

WOMAN....

MAN. Sorry. I do this. I... See, I really do think your lips are beautiful but not in a... y'know. Not like that. Like if you were looking at a piece of sculpture in a gallery or something. Some old thing made out of marble or – not that you're old or anything, I don't mean... I mean a thing of beauty, y'know? Like the *Pietà*. Or the *Venus de Milo*. Like that. But I do that. I say things. And then I know I should've just thought them so... I'll just think it instead.

WOMAN. I'd rather you didn't.

MAN. Eh?

WOMAN. Think it. I'd rather you didn't.

MAN. Oh.

Beat.

Not bad thoughts. Nice ones –

WOMAN. I don't know you.

MAN. So I have to not think things 'cause you don't know me?

Pause.

Very strange weather, very unseasonal. Ice on the wings is
no good. Neither is a bird in the engine. Or lightning. Ever
thought about lightning? Nah. Don't trust it all so easily.
Not as trusting as you.

WOMAN. You don't know me.

Pause.

MAN. Life's short. I know that much.

Beat.

Could both die out there today.

Beat.

It flips (*Indicates stomach.*) when I look at you.

Beat.

Or should I just have thought that?

Beat.

Too late now.

*She looks at him, then picks up her bag and exits. He sits
there for a moment. He ponders on what to do next. Then he
picks up his bag and follows her out.*

Darkness.

A Nick Hern Book

Abigail first published in Great Britain in 2017 as a paperback original by Nick Hern Books Limited, The Glasshouse, 49a Goldhawk Road, London W12 8QP, in association with The Bunker, London

Abigail copyright © 2017 Fiona Doyle

Fiona Doyle has asserted her moral right to be identified as the author of this work

Cover photograph by Jasper Soloff

Designed and typeset by Nick Hern Books, London
Printed in the UK by Mimeo Ltd, Huntingdon, Cambridgeshire PE29 6XX

A CIP catalogue record for this book is available from the British Library

ISBN 978 1 84842 648 1